A gener[ ]   hip

persons would reach maturity, filling

filling the Western world with cosmology,

renaissance dichotomy & principles of

extended thinking.

    The full flowers of the crop, freshly

planted would spring forth, apply-

ing the experimental processes of the

mid-20ᵗʰ century to the burgeoning

problems of the 21st.

    Telegraphy, montage will be the

harmonies of ~~design~~ environment and

design — The cities will be puri-

fied of extremes in stability, and

the movements of essential diversity

A book of PROPHECIES

A book of PROPHECIES

John Wieners

Edited by Michael Carr
with an Introduction by Jim Dunn

BOOTSTRAP PRESS

© Copyright was instituted under Henry VIII. Please credit author and publisher in all quotations, etc., and let us know where to look for same.

First published 2007

Bootstrap Productions
82 Wyman Street
Lowell, MA 01852

Bootstrap Press is an imprint of Boostrap Productions, Inc., a non-profit arts and literary collective founded by Derek Fenner and Ryan Gallagher.

Cover design by Derek Fenner.
Cover photo of John Wieners by unknown photographer; unknown date.
Author photo by Allen de Loach; Buffalo, New York 1970.
Printed and bound in the US by McNaughton & Gunn.

ISBN 978-0-9779975-4-5

This publications was made possible by donations to Bootstrap Productions Incorporated. Please visit our online catalogue and consider helping us support contemporary arts and literary culture.

Bootstrap Productions
www. bootstrapproductions.com

Distributed to the trade by Small Press Distribution

THIS IS A BOOTSTRAP PRODUCTION!

Introduction

John Wieners is as clear to me today, in thought and feeling, as he was those days sitting in the guest room of his Beacon Hill apartment by the window overlooking the African Meetinghouse, smoking a Kent, whispering to himself, as thoughts and memories danced behind his electric blue eyes. His voice with that soft, sonorous timbre and South Shore Boston lilt still echoes in my mind especially when reading his words. His impeccable manners and eloquence are as memorable as his voice. Beneath his gentle nature there was an ironclad will and determination to be his own master at all times. His loyalty to his own artistic path often seemed contradictory to the ambition of most poets for recognition, awards, and general acclaim. John was *Garbo-esque* in his determination to live singularly of his own accord. He was often opaque, cryptic, and mysterious to those who approached him in person with particular expectations for him to be the mythic *poète maudit*. His surrealistic monologues were poetry in and of themselves. He would rattle off non sequiturs, unconnected phrases and seemingly unrelated facts and observations. They served in part as a defense mechanism, but other times they were simply his perceptions of daily life. After an all-night trip from Boston to Philadelphia, I asked John what he thought of my driving skills. He replied, "Oh, the popcorn was tour de force. Did we stop for the dogs on the outskirts of town?" Although I had no idea what he was talking about, I never forgot it. Wieners followed his own whim and fancy with a religious devotion. The friends who slipped under his curtain of white noise and unconditionally accepted the man behind the shattered mirror trusted in his ability to know what he was doing even when he appeared to be completely befuddled and befuddling. He also possessed a great sense of humor and an impeccable sense of timing, which helped him survive the cruel irony of being one of the master poets of our time, forced to live week-to-week in abject poverty.

Many times I watched John silently meditating on the edge of his single bed or a bed in a hotel room, as he traveled within his mind to some distant time or particular memory. His hands would dance as if conducting a secret symphony. He would whisper gently as he transported himself musically and magically from memory to memory. It was beautiful to witness, but it seemed to be an intensely personal experience. I often felt like I was intruding in the presence of such an introspective voyage. John's sensibilities did not allow him any psychic distance from the specific emotions of his memories. There was no separation between his dreams and reality, no distance between his memory of love and the pain of its loss. Although his reality was often bleak, he was surprisingly content, because his dreams were only a blink away. His poems were invocations, prayers recited to himself. As his lyric became more cryptic, his obsessive duty to his writing continued as he spilled his poetry out onto everything from shopping lists to advertising supplements. With much of John's writing he was mirroring his thoughts and feelings exactingly, into poetry of particular personal drama. His poetry directly mapped his heart and mind, a yearning yet always loving heart, and a mind of a million mirrors each reflecting a vision of their own world; each world of its own space, time, and feeling. He wrote religiously until his death, but much of his later writing remains undiscovered, or lost forever.

Now, unexpectedly, out of nowhere, five years after his death, a treasure trove of writings has been discovered. Written thirty-six years ago when Wieners was thirty-six years old, it spans the years 1970-1972 between the publication of *Nerves* and *Behind the State Capitol or Cincinnati Pike*. It includes a few previously published poems but for the most part it contains unpublished and undiscovered pieces. This book will take a prominent place in the canon of Wieners' work, providing a vital link between the more cohesive lyric of *Nerves* and the fragmentary surrealistic visions of *Behind The State Capitol*. Wieners penned the title *A Book of PROPHECIES* himself in the front of the journal. He places specific emphasis on the word "PROPHECIES" by writing it out in all capital letters. The prophetic tone to some of the pieces is nowhere more apparent than in the first poem in the journal, titled amazingly "2007." Wieners' vision of 2007 is infused with the positive prediction of a society of hip persons reaching maturity, filling the world with "cosmology, renaissance dichotomy & principles of extended thinking." His vision of a more perfect and harmonious society is reiterated later in the untitled poem that begins "On the era of a new age..." His surreal, utopian dream did not come to fruition, but his vision is courageously optimistic, launching into the surreal. It is the vision of a poet dreaming of the next century while living through the personally turbulent days of the late sixties and early seventies. His prescient eye and lyric ear poised towards the future are astounding for their insight and detail. Throughout the journal, Wieners delivers the prophetic and the profane, the future through the portals of the past, love through the broken heart of loss, family through the awkward silences of parental and sibling tensions, and pure lyrical poetry through the longing desires of an artist not afraid to create beautiful gems and give them away freely.

The early seventies was a transitional, yet productive time in Wieners' life. He was living in a suburban colonial on a tree-lined cul-de-sac with his mother and father behind the Hanover Mall on the South Shore of Boston. It would be a few years before he would settle into his Beacon Hill apartment on Joy Street. Familial tension is one aspect of the drama against which many of these poems and dreams are forged. During this time his mentor Charles Olson, his friend Stephen Jonas, and his mother Anna Laffan Wieners passed away. His evocation of the influence of Olson and his mother on his life and work is one of many amazing pieces contained in the journal. Wieners pays tribute to his mother and Olson by contrasting their generous, loving, artistic temperament with the cold and distant nature of his father, Albert. In the balance between the stark reality of his father and the poetic gifts of his greatest influence, Wieners and his mother stand united with Olson in John's mind. In honest, unflinching prose Wieners contrasts the love of Olson as "a thinker, a man skilled in letters and history, who had no patience with excess" to his own father, who "believed in analysis...who persists in domination of each instant, the horror and agony of his family." Also, the stunning prose poem "The Problem of Madness" courageously confronts the darkness that shadowed him throughout his life. "Yes, the thirst is upon me. For breaking out of the shell, at thirty-six years, for shedding the chrysalis, and becoming the man Jung predicted." Light and darkness sway back and forth throughout the journal. The poet follows the light of his inspiration beyond the limitations of his daily existence, to the future, fearlessly writing his poetic prophecies in soft syllables of sweet lyric and intensely personal poetry.

Because of Wieners' unstable mental state during this period, *A Book of PROPHECIES* is both fascinating and disturbing, nowhere more so than in the poems that deal with his feelings toward Robert Creeley. Wieners' affection for Creeley over the decades of their acquaintance was strong and unwavering. Even in his later journals he dedicated certain poems "pour mon amour, Bob Creeley." However in his poem "For Robert Creeley" the darker side of his delirious feelings for Creeley is expressed in poetic terms. His portrayal of Creeley as a "one eyed inventor in his imagination," "dark haired dabbler in agnosticism," "fucking the women with bloody assholes," "a eunuch by the turn of the century," "Eating brains in retaliation for excess, living in the past for revenge," is honest in raw emotion reflected in the rough light of unrequited love. Creeley also is the implied king of the poem "Taking king to bed with me." In this poem Wieners incorrectly predicts Robin Blaser's death in 2006, and imagines his sister as Princess Victoria Adelaide of Schleswig-Holstein, married to the King of Poland, but raped in a wedding gown by Wieners' imagined king, Creeley. The heart of the poem is the pain and frustration felt by Wieners from loving Creeley, a friend and fellow poet, who loves many women, but does not love Wieners in the same way. If Creeley, the lower case king of the poem's title, will not go to bed with Wieners, then Wieners' desire, will and imagination make it true within the poem, "Mr. Creeley a handsome, dashing, Lothario of enormous talent is thought by me as a mate for release."

Five years. Thirty-six years. Seventy-two years. John Wieners had his own measure, outside of time. Through the magic of his poetry, within the force of his imagination, he was able to traverse time, layering his beautiful words over the memories of his rugged life. Poetry was John's vessel of God, and through this vessel he was the commander of time across lonely distances, through the exertion of the sheer force of his will and desire. Wieners once described poets as wraiths who cross time. The image of poet as a ghostly apparition casting himself into the future while anchored to the longings and desires of the past is an integral one that Wieners evokes many times in his work. The poet as wraith is reminiscent of the image Walt Whitman evokes in "Crossing Brooklyn Ferry," traversing the waters of time on the Brooklyn Ferry to the shores of future readership where he would become one with a new generation of readers; an audience that eluded him in his own times. "And you that shall cross from shore to shore years hence, are more to me, and more in my meditations, than you might suppose." Wieners' desire to connect with any audience was more complicated than Whitman's. His relationship to his work is at the heart of his contradiction as an artist; he wrote heartbreakingly beautiful lyrics to past lovers and future readers, without particular concern if the work reached an audience at all.

The journal also includes fascinating, detailed lists of poets he had met, gifts his mother gave him, women he had known, and a list of clothes and fashion accessories that eventually takes off into the realm of John's poetic imagination. The lists are a valuable compendium to the poems in the book. Wieners' unique and brilliant sense of infusing mundane facts with a magical and fantastic flair is abundant in these lists. It is a technique that he would employ with even greater vigor in later journals. However, the heart of this book is the depth of quality and the number of new poems that make this collection such a rare and beautiful find.

It is no small miracle that such an important work has been preserved, and discovered. Circumstances have aligned themselves now for this book to come forth into the world. As the echo of Wieners' classic defensive reply for new work – "Let's hold off on this for awhile" – grows fainter, the writing itself demands to be held onto now and be heard by new generations of readers who delight in his masterful lyrical powers. As with many things associated with Wieners, the provenance of the journal is storied and interesting. Wieners gave the journal directly to Louisa Solano, friend and former proprietor of the Grolier Poetry Bookshop in Cambridge, Massachusetts. The dedication to her is the last entry in the journal.

Louisa passed the journal to Robert Wilson of the Phoenix Book Shop. The journal was then in a private collection for a number of years before it was sold by Christie's in May, 1991 to Thomas A. Goldwasser Rare Books. Goldwasser sold the journal to the Kent State University Department of Special Collections and Archives in December, 1991, where it has remained ever since. The poet, Michael Carr, discovered the journal listed online in 2005 while searching for Wieners' archived papers. He wrote to Kent State for a copy. Cara Gilgenbach of the Special Collections and Archives Department delivered a full photocopy of the journal to Mick in August, 2005. Carr has worked since then, transcribing and deciphering Wieners' handwritten entries into this edition. He is the sole reason this journal is now published. Without his dedication, enthusiasm, and fortitude, as well the assistance and access afforded by Cara Gilgenbach and Kent State University, this journal would have remained neglected like so many other writings of this unique and beloved poet.

Jim Dunn
Boston, MA
January 2007

Note on the Text

This book is a transcription of the contents of one of John Wieners' manuscript journals, attempting faithfulness to the handwritten original while bringing it to the printed page. Some poems have been reformatted for wider margins where, for example, in the journal longer lines were dropped from lack of space. Edits marked on the text by Wieners have for the most part been changed as he indicated. There are a few pages included in facsimile only, as they much better communicate the complexity of the originals than any possible transcription would. The spelling throughout is Wieners' own.

Acknowledgements

For their helpful insight and encouragement many thanks are due to Jim Dunn, Raymond Foye, Charley Shively, Gerrit Lansing, Alan Davies and Derek Fenner. Gratitude to Cara Gilgenbach at Kent State University's Department of Special Collections and Archives. And thanks to Heather Pawlak, Allen De Loach's stepdaughter, for kind permission to reproduce the photos of John Wieners.

A.W.S. G. "Look up Roy L. Dunkee

Crosby, Co.

phone number in Frankfort

May 21, 1926

Mrs advised in. 1929.
long June 6. 1929.

John Mullaney 19107
1958

John Joseph LeFran
66. 6

acceptation
San Francisco

died 1958 - May 16

Baker Memorial Hospital
726 - 2000 = Room 1014
Mr Albert E. Wienis Sr.

It cannot come from
the tissues, it must come
from the person.

E.(The)
Gardner
Fry
6

2. Anandia in Roxbury
Anndumas

I left him in 1953
w/ 17 Drury St
I havent seen Jim
since 1953 —
no R.P. pictures

We have never Discussed relations of his sexual nature since~

A book of P R O P H E C I E S

A generation of new, advanced hip persons would reach maturity, filling the Western world with cosmology, renaissance dichotomy & principles of extended thinking.

The full flowers of the crop, freshly planted would spring forth, applying the experimental processes of the mid-20th century to the burgeoning problems of the 21st.

Telegraphy, montage will be the harmonies of environment and design. The cities will be purified of extremes in stability, and the movements of essential diversity will promote renewed peace and perceptive pleasure. Programs will be less theoretical and provide for adventurous paths to be everyday pursuits in the accepted patterns of existence.

Imagination will be more pervasive and progress made in travel over ocean and space. Dress asymetrical and modes of greeting and conversation elliptical and extreme Bizareness absent except in bigness, mamoth grandeur of architecture and color. Music string and forms of verse controlled symbolism.

With Meaning

Rise, shining martyrs,
over the multitudes
for the season of migration
between earth and heaven.

Rise shining martyrs, cut down in fire
and darkness, speeding past light
straight through imagination's park.

In the smart lofts of West Newton St.
or the warehouse district of S.F., come,
let us go back to bequeathed memory

of Columbus Ave, or the beach at the end of Polk St.,
where Jack Spicer went, or Steve Jonas' apts. all over town
from Beacon Hill to St. Charles, without warning, how they went.

The multitude of martyrs, staring out of
town houses now on Delaware Ave. in the grey mist
of traffic circles, taking LSD, then not coming back

to rooming houses, Berkeley and motorcycles.
Books of poems all we had to bound the frustration
of leaving them behind, in Millbrook mornings on the swing
with Tambimuttu, excercising his solar plexus, during conversation.

Each street contains its own time of other decades,
recollected after the festival, carefully, as so many
bright jewels to brush aside for present occupation.

A printing press by the Pacific, a Norman cottage in the east,
dancing to Donovan, in Pucci pajamas, or perhaps, prison past
                              imagination's plain,
with Saturday night sessions in the tombs. Oh yes,

rise, shining martyrs, out of the moviehouse's matinee
on Long Island, to your love walking by in the sun.
Over the multitudes, endless shortripping.

And backyard swimming pools of Arizona
and Pacific Palisades, in the canyons of LA, plus the journeys
over oceans, and islands, to metropolis spreadeagled the earth.

Yes, rise shining martyrs,
out of your graves, to tell us
what to do, read your poems
with the eyes of young men,
in springtime moon light.
Rise and salvage our century.

Never Put Anything In Writing

His laugh was imbecilic
sounded across the room, unbelievably
looking at the Jackie Gleason show, continuously

as a woman's across the sand, creeping
to the sea, in darkness, or lascivously
self-indulgently, like

Imagination dies and is replaced by thought, or is it regret. Hair falls out, and grows no more.

I remember watching old movies of the forties and romanticizing about the glamour of night, and cheap hotels, the thrill of electric light, under street lamps. Yes, New York is dead, as it once was, peopled by phantoms now who struggle along city streets, the color of dumps and warehouses.

Yes the movies of a generation ago changed the metropolis of my dreams, believing in candlelight dinners, small cafés and stringed instruments, waltzing the world away. And love, too. That all consumption could be found in a kiss.

Speeding away to the mountains for a weekend.

Under the Moon

When will love come
with all the dreams
I have worshipped, again

indiscriminately, love
its players blind, stalks in
without being asked

takes us in its arms for a little while,
then lets us drop, after so short a time,
leaving us broken, weeping on stones.

After the sunlit afternoons, what then,
the midnight paramours, in fleabag tenements,
oh yes, what then is left to do, where to go?

Oh god, what has become of me, where is the self
that used to flock to bars, always seeking
for the partner, gone, turned away.

Then it happened, all of a sudden, you were there
in various guises, on the dance floor, in the back room,
piercing the gloom with cigarettes, movie theatres,

and theatre stubs, always alone, you were there,
after the theatre, greeting me in the lobby, on the elevator.

Now we are alone, in separate parts, and countries.
Who will bring us together again?

Most of my love life has been spent in longing
yet you the most real of all, and the shortest, remain

to haunt the penthouses, and chaumieres, with champagne
and three course dinners.

                    THEN
                You have a melody,
                            that is the waltz
that imbues sex with meaning and love. Standing before the hearth,
in pink and black pajamas, with a light behind your head,
when you speak, or extending your knees backward to the log fire
I built, for the first time, arriving in the middle of the night
by cab, to the deserted chalet we rented for the summer.

How sweet it was, an ideal situation for us to bloom through
                                        love's care.
Yes, our health was bad, and we had too much money.
Keeping away from town, without car, or phone, or clock.

Our luck, to run out of
                what was it?
You had other things to do, other places to be, other men to love.
And I was not enough, you were my first

After Reading Words

~~What can I s~~

What can I, may I, can I say to you,
the competition of one man against another.

Your impeccable ear will never die
on the page. Your ear for phrase —

and let the mind drop off to
another concern. It will never return

without concentration, ~~concern~~ your self
awareness of the process happening

drowns in the flood of my own nature,
rising to express feeling for you,

the music of wholeness through ~~feeling~~ having
something to say, strong examination

                                          return
of person, situation and ~~strength~~;
inventive, intense and interior

After Reading <u>Words</u>

What can I, may I, <u>can</u> I say to you,
the competition of one man against another.

Your impeccable ear will never die
on the page. Your ear for phrase—

and let the mind drop off to
another concern. It will never return

without concentration, your self
awareness of the process happening

drowns in the flood of my own nature,
rising to express feeling for you,

the music of wholeness through having
something to say, strong examination

of person, situation and return;
inventive, intense and interior

Sexual Despair

loneliness, despite record of Charles Aznavour
chantent in the Paris 40's, how far is it
to friendship, to the sea side where past loves reside.

oh who will
dispell mel-
ancholy

        from this Sunday
        in the country.

I am wrapped around by
           memory

and thoughts of death, alone.
I need you, my little son

to be beside me in bed
jerking your meat and
smoking hash-hish.

          What will the future bring
          this fear ling-

          ers every day,
          without going away,

despite the big band,
      the glad hand,
the thousand grands
in the bank account.

Lights on in the daytime
all friends gone out

perhaps fate or language
shall draw together the strands

to land us as lovers, someone
I have in mind,

        who will release
        this frustration, this longing

I have tried other men,
they do not help.

        I cannot even eat
        and would rather be alone.

But it is no good.
I once believed in God,

        and at least knew
        I was doing wrong.

That was something, a song,
a sore to cure.

        But now it is only defeat
        before one has even begun.

Spring's woe, gestation
creates this condition

        every year as tiny buds
        sprout on trees.

Lend me a lover, this year
I fear,

may be my last, alone.
From now on,

it will be together, with someone
if I have to go to the North Pole
for satisfaction. One March, I found
the crown of golden love, and seek still
its owner. It should be a time of
new beginning, new hopes, new desire.
I pace around the room as a caged beast
and know it will be no easy answer
this time, no sudden meeting on a river bank for ten minutes.
I need something else, now, I need you, whoever you may be,
                                     to fill this need.
And I have two men in mind, I could be happy with,

                to wake up with, and know
I would be with them, for the day, make them food,
   and watch their dark faces
       through the living room.

After reading <u>Second Avenue</u>
For Frank O'Hara

As a jar of Tibetan snow, you melted
in mid-summer, without worry or woe,
laughing a way out of disaster
to mock its undertow. Even though some

of your friends have gone ahead
to arrange celebrations for the occasion
and some gone since, who
toasted you on arrival, out of frustration

with us here, yes, your heroes paved a way,
divinities of cosmopolitan incline.
Names unforgotten, faces etched in blond gravure,
how may we exist, though know your words endure.

2.

A certain sense of city behavior
existed within us, which has
slowly crumbled away since
we haven't seen you for years,

at the New School, or standing dinner
in Moo Gai's on Second Avenue.
I can't call you by telephone

or mourn the fact you went to Fire Island
for a long weekend, leaving me ruffled
with absence, at a movie on the East Side,

or a cocktail party at Morris Golde's.
You were so kind to me,
when I first had lox, other delicacies.

No there'll be no more gossip of movie stars,
as you have written so well
but this is dangerous, I know

and beers at Joe's, above Die Wurst Haus,
no more mourning, and nasal inflection.
Some tone of the town gone, some society curse.

3.

Language has power to clap its lid on a poet,
control our lives suddenly, as lovers we find
ourselves together in a Turkish bath, I never went
that time you asked; I don't know why.

We were together. One must submit to speech,
words when we were together, in South Station.
You shall be forever in my heart. Behind my eye lids,
I have your books, your mouth to remember me as well.

à Charles Trenet, poete

How many times, when my mind
had nothing to do, I put on your record
and found myself in another mood.

Yes, this will do, this is good, your
delicate voice as a youth
                                 in a back bedroom
out of Brooklyn, posing under a
                                      lintel, naked.

    Jazz violin, through the midnight
    as the voice of my wife-to-be
                                  squeaks as a
                    bird in the yard.

And Language of Conversation

Bottles of scent on a bureau,
the smiling face of a friend,
abandoned in time,

     these lend pleasure to boredom,
     inflicted on children by their parents,
     who never ignited creation except

          through their loving; imagination
          straightarmed by age.
                    What hope
          awaits the future but labor, the actual

attention to meditation upon conditions
of peace, tranquility and nature: alone.
Yes, love beckons still as the moon

     on September noons when moonsoon
     torrents descended on the Patients' Club
     in Central Islip, I would sit under the tin

          roofs, a bundle of nerves and wish
          for nothing more than this; my own room
          and parents outside, asleep in the gloom.

The problem of madness

has to be dealt with seriously, in our time for we have not advanced so greatly from days of the pit and Bedlam. There are problems in every human person and some take more advanced manifestation in individuals, with particular advantages and drawbacks.

There are men with genetic weakness, physical defects, aggressive attitudes and fearful displays of manner. In their own families, if they have them, and too many mental patients are without kin of any sort, these faults are taken for granted and usually the result of a domineering mother.

They diminish the term 'madness' from being applicable to a person for life. Yet there are other violent examples, and damages to the central and autonomic nervous systems from drinking, smoking and drugs, that can be cured through cellular therapy, rest and blood cleansing. Madness may not be applied here, though ill-temper is.

What then is madness? Simply disgruntlement, hostility, aggression such as war, then ours is a mad century.

Unpleasant experiences one is unable to forget, disappointments in love, physicality, longing, frustration, sexuality, these all produce disease.

Good looks taken for granted, muscularity, well-endowed proportions, all become bored in time, unless seen through other's eyes, as this too is known as schizophrenia; or empathy in the theatre and negative capability though verse.

Yes, one writes, out of dedication, habit and need. One longs to be recognized. One has aspiration and ambition, and impulse to improve himself continually. One hopes for stability. And yet in pursuit of security, within his own desire, one has applied the word "mad" by society, at the bidding of an opposite-countered family, towards materialism, adultery, provincialism and drunkeness, then how is one to behave, and be believed by his contemporaries, except as a freak or aberration. Even though doctored through affection and faithfulness.

2

These too go hand-in-hand with ignorance and unquestioned habit. One must improve his concerns, not with the emphereal, unless in a responsive, creative romantic realization of imaginative strivings. If I sound like John Hall Wheelock here, and use all the hogwash of aesthetic cliché, let me explain that this is the only way one may rid himself of such trappings. I have lost my memory through drugs. I have regained it by going back to school and studying the same things over again. I have regained it by examining the artifacts of the past, and was frightened by seizing upon them as objects from another person. Such they were, as the metabolic change inflicted by drugs, is true. And a real one. One never gets over.

III

Yes, the thirst is upon me. For breaking out of the shell, at thirty-six years, for shedding the chrysalis, and becoming the man Jung predicted. Not the <u>Fellini</u> <u>Satyricon</u>. I had that as a youth. But the measured arbiter of verses. And moods. And passion. And poetics.

Form is a non-continuum. It changes from person to person. It changes with time. It is non-absolute.

Each content is different. It adheres to person as a product of different time and place, race and language.

> I am no Greek, hath
> not the advantage. No Roman
> neither, etc.

Yet one may not simply celebrate the differences. There are continuities, congruences in time, from far places, estranged persons. May one call these similarities, and produce a notion of text from them. May one develop wisdom and be accepted by his friends, no more than fate, one has earned through hardihood?

What reward for the well-ordered line, or the years spent, devotedly worshipping an ideal. The dedication of applying art to every-day existence. In place of commonplace enterprise, it is heroic. Or non-thinking employment, through boorish exposition of authority, the humble practice of verse, art, individual expression, assumes sureness of loveliness.

When men are lovely, why dont they see it's in they share common attitudes. Each man is capable of being an artist. Of formulating artistic principles in time. Some resist out of being stubborn. But their dreams are evident, aspiration too strong a condition to disguise, try as they may, though religion to provide a pat answer.

Yes, some men may go on, out of heroism. Some, most die for their attempts. Their push drives them into all areas of exploration. Not only in form, but formlessness. One waits for print, as an anchor, an offer to arrive each afternoon in the mail, to fulfill for what effect other than one is doing what he has chosen to do. And one has succeeded at it, then no one accepts this but himself, through the vision of his loved one.

Supposition

And after you're gone,
will I be unhappy
staring catatonically
out the bus window,
a victim ~of too many
cigarettes, letters unanswered,
poems unread?

Will I able to
cope, hope that ~~these only~~ only
lonely days are gone,
on my own at last
my own boss. Unable to
call you if I wanted to,
with no one to turn to
for help, unable to

make even one mistake,
left by memory.

Supposition

And after you're gone,
will I be unhappy
staring catatonically
out the bus window,
a victim of too many
cigarettes, letters unanswered,
poems unread?

Will I be able to
cope, hope that only
lonely days are gone,
on my own at last
my own boss. Unable to
call you if I wanted to,
with no one to turn to
for help, unable to

make even one mistake,
reft by memory.

Our inchoate love

Bequest

I see her sleeping in the chair,
slipping away each day without care,
acquiring a habit she never had before
of passing time not as shrew but in despair.

Heartless it is to die this way
with nothing one may do to allay
her time, away from the grave.

Oh, if there were only something I could do,
to erase from my heart the rue
of seeing her this way, sleep in sorrow.

A life unfullifilled, or so I think,
plagued with a man, sodden in drink
for centuries, a Tuetonic link

to Northern Ireland, who does not act
the part of husband very often, or father
either, nonetheless she loves him, or rather
I gather this as I watch her

Eyes light up when she speaks of him, but when
he comes home, it's pride; there is no life between
them, nonetheless a kind of bickering exists
I take it as remnants of their great romance

I know they had; as I had once, before I gave up
and turned away from hope, to other men,
or drugs, thus the cycle goes on, if only there were some
redemption, at the end, besides the memory of children.

Take not from me the dreams of youth,
let my flesh go, but not its dreams,
take my parents too, but let my dreams alone.

Adolescence

Take not from me the dreams of my youth,
take my flesh away, but let my dreams alone
take not the desire of youth, the high hope, ambition

they were not mine to keep, but pass now to others then
let them go, let me be left utterly alone and bereft.
It does not matter, the sun shines down where before was the moon.

O! the treason of inversion that twists meaning
when what I wanted to say was the moon shines down now
where before was the sun on stained glass windows
in the library at Boston College, where I pledged to poetry.
It does not matter, though I have forgotten the reason
why I should go on, wanting him now, for my own in place of
                              fame or shame or wisdom.

Drive Under the Moon

What is this listlessness that bows my head,
that sends me hours early to bed
And makes me dread

The anxiety that seeps through my limbs,
Knowing I only will think of him
As I do every evening, or her

It makes little difference, sir,
for both lead to some disaster
of longing the bitter
              End, without meaning or madness
only, alone, under the moon, more than both.
                   Oh, I am sloth,

        and would go, run amuck through the woods,
        as we need to, in Annisquam, I after him,
        as he does now, with his wife the winner.

<u>Maps</u> - Oppen, George
        Jackson Mac Low
        John Wieners
        <u>Wm Bronk</u>

8 pages =
6 or 7 =
———————————————

John Taggart
Box 135
Newbury, Pa. 17240

———————————————
 Wilson College =

<u>Athaneum/</u>
    Richelieu

 how he

On My Father's Chair

The May-star from afar
ploughs morning bales

to tread March's last days,
too easy to forget

how sweet she went,
while I sit here

lost in a haze, gazing across
at her, in liberation at last.

Don't Explain ✓

Just a way to get by,
to have what you want, a front
to a back, perhaps to remembered.

I wont ask you again.
you I recall, with

any fall, I shall un burdened
by hunger or fatigue underground,
as a network

of cavernous glow. Aloud mouth
to a an immigrant ignoramus,

asking questions of a diseased man,
with the same blood as ours.

Don't Explain

Just a way to get by,
to have what you want, a front
to a back, perhaps remembered.

I wont ask you again,
you I recall, with

any fall, unburdened
by hunger or fatigue underground,
as a network

of cavernous glow. A loud mouth
to an immigrant ignoramus,

asking questions of a diseased man,
with the same blood as ours.

A Lincoln Rocker

I thought I'd die, too
along with you
why should I care
as stricken, madonna
of the streets.

> Confused, grey patterns
> in the abyss of exile
> against the cement wall
> opposed to wood.

There's nothing wrong with that.
You're only a ranch hand.

I died no one
as [I once felt I [had
to be someone.

So sour am I on April
my inspiration not good enough.

To Robert Creeley

He causes trouble in the Anglo-Saxon camp
fucking the women with bloody assholes,
one-eyed inventor in his imagination,
like Willa Mae on Main Street,
a enuch by the turn of the century.

Eating brains in retaliation for excess,
living in the past for revenge. A black haired dabbler
in agnosticism, hurling the taunts of an adulteress toward
                                                her brother,
hating the love of two men together.

Don't send me away
You are so important
What can you be doing talking
        to your selflessness.
It's so important.

I Still Love You

Because when I fade out
you're still there
as mine as no one ever was.

Just Perfect Now

The man who went away
lives to return another day,
haunting the railway, causing
anxiety and vanity to mar
eternity by his search for
fulfillment in a poet's arms.

How exciting to share naivete,
the grand experience of being wanted
when the world spills its fusion through
the metropolis of perfection.
It's make no difference at distance

or loss despite achievement. Forbears resurrect intimacy
which remains isolate, the holding on,
the recognition's entrance, in devotion,
to pursue their path's plans.
For history and importance.

If I thought I could benefit
one's man life that would
be enough.

Now, they can keep their business to themselves.

A rainy dawn in Scollay Square
~~outside~~ the Rialto Theatre,
driven out by hirelings
hypnotized with ~~the~~ past leaders

the blue mist crept up Hanover Street
down Cambridge Street over the hump
of ~~Beacon~~ hill,
at the corner ~~onto~~ the Charles River
horizon —
~~that~~ sense of unfolding charisma

pressed one ~~was~~ on to contemplate
~~the~~ our Swiss pendulum — of transience
and permanency, between the variety
of markets and fire stations with doors
open, that wait
for those who hesitate or investigate.
the name of Boston, Charlestown, with Lynn.

1-17-1971

To a cartographer, Glenda Farrell.

Now, they can keep their business to themselves.

A rainy dawn in Scollay Square
outside the Rialto Theatre
driven out by hirelings
hypotized with past leaders

the blue mist crept up Hanover Street
down Cambridge Street over the hump of Beacon hill,
at the corner onto the Charles River horizon—
that sense of unfolding charisma

pressed one on to contemplate
our Swiss pendulum of transience
and permanecy, between the variety
of markets and fire stations with doors open, that wait
for those who hesitate or investigate
the name of Boston, Charlestown, with Lynn.

1-17-1971
To a cartographer, Glenda Farrell.

Pollution
Natural Resourses
Transportation
Poverty

Saturday Afternoon

after films

To find a wife, after thirty years
waiting and desirous, since the first day
beside the pond, when he pledged me

to observe, cherish and reverence
the man, my love, that youth romantic,
who is more handsome than anyone

in faith and body, his perfection possessed me
to follow him as best I could, from May 1940
until the present, May 1970, when we went

to the theater again, as friends, before our friends
in the lobby, outside talking as strangers,
tradition fulfilled itself by our meeting.

A supper, a walk to the bus
through the square, a pride
in ourselves, despite dissimiliarity —,

a stop at the market and exchange
of desire led to increased passion
cut short by my husband's distaste

for my permanence, which I inflicted on him
against his will, at times, other times, he submitted to me
as an original need. We shared one hour and a half

recognizing identities of style and forms.
Simultaneity was not achieved, though we wished for it
in different ways of combination. How we saw each

through the afternoon, as progressive towards
perhaps the future unity, visually, physically,
in domestic relation.

5. Call Dave
Dukee's parent came,
tell them Thurston's
up here masquerading
as my father.

6. 4 yrs ago, he's 67.

Armstrong
1.

[signature]
2.

Susan Hayward

3.

Yes, there is a state and it will punish you for denying it

You have a kidney mind

Alexander Calder

1930 Harrow

We Would Be Two Men

After eleven years
of ambition and frustration,
expending desire on poets,
attending readings, giving benefits,
burdened by malnutrition,

a strange fire burst between
myself and a dark-eyed man,
who was married but whom I later
discovered to be my husband,
a gentleman skilled in business and letters.

He is wealthy, gay, and drives cars,
having accomplished achievement
in theatre, music, and medecine.
He travels from continent to continent
at times accompanied with women and children,
addressing no one but myself.

Lost in his arms for two days,
I find my secret passions rewarded,
receiving kisses as from a king of the Black Sea,
no one able to compete with his necessity.

L   Fel
P   <u>Jeanette Lerman</u>

1 – at <u>1 o'clock</u>

12 o'clock bus
——
Black Mountain College –
Neat and orderly –
Well-organized

Taking king to bed with me

in preference to 75 women – a royal imposter named of Robin Blaser
2006 – the day he died.

They'll open up the earth with you and wash the heads of the
women my man sleeps with named of Rose Robert White.

If I am in love with a man who sleeps with other women then I shall
forget him. My sister Victoria Scheswig-Holstein married to the
King of Poland, has been raped by my king; in a wedding gown.

A man who gives me no pleasure in such recollection. I am stunned.
My brother arranges such torment in his affair with M.E. Bassett.

Tom Cassidy in Iran with whom I have been consumated refers to
my king as crown. How I need him, want him, request him by mail,
phone, and in person, as poet, friend and husband.

Norman to Pict.
Peter as fellow =
Catherine in blue lids, white pearls, and glass.
I remain in 1944 the sodomitic delight of my true nature.

The how-could-you daddy interuption of her step-dghtr. K.H.
Creeley is best returned by marriage to her own father, Clay B Shaw
of Storrs, Connecticut.

Mr. Creeley, a handsome, dashing, Lothario of enormous talent is
thought by me as a mate for release. His other needs of course of
menial, repitition and independence are best suited to the temper of
a loving warm, and human woman, with whom he lives, a girl I met
when young, with her mother, and named B.L. Hall. She remains as
wife, housekeeper and bastion. Elizabeth Jones; Dolly Madison mis-
tress to James. Rudolph, and Polly and Trudy Tedford.

<u>I am one thing & one man.</u> An ant crawling across the stove, a silver knife on a plate with butter, a book of poems on the cabinet, two cigarette butts, masked in a sauce of ashes. Edward VI to George V.

<u>Mad about each rise in separate houses, in different clothes,</u> keeping our minds focused in such facts, despite the rudeness of unwarranted inattention, the disclosure of womanly infidelity becomes a bore, for as many women this man confesses to me, continue to remain in pain.

     <u>Thus he receives eight whacks</u> as they are raped against their will. Eight guillotines will remind him of his broken vows.
    Minor Values

Susan Maria Theresa of the man James, has been shocked for the last time at her father's infidelity. H.R.H. Rudolph of the Imperial & Royal House of Amble Plains has returned as my support to Charles – new & last Libation to grace the behavior of our family
    James Dorherty my only husband still haunts the pages of <u>history</u>.

Poem for A Reading June 10th
at Boston University

A drunken father sits
in the living room, con-
templating stock on Sat-

urday, while his middle son
works at diamonds and plat-
inum in the den below,

listening to Jerome Kern and
dreaming of desert wind,
whistling by the window.

Too much alcohol, too many rel-
atives, too few lovers to last
out the fraud of vorticism.

The passage of two writers beyond
the room where he hears
a solitary romance, issuing

upon the pine buds fruit.
No exile, nor mellow discontent
requires retribution against

the failure of premeditation to provide
redemption for an honored guide,
upon the faults of society suicide.

2

The younger brother resumes
offenses under the guise of
interest, excessively con-

spicuos through repeated
insults directed without
purpose in this place,

where flowers wither, birds
cry threats beside swamps,
in human form rake lawns

with reason of suspicion.
The blossoms within our breasts
shoot scarlet poor maroon.

For Julie.

A Coffee and two Doughnuts

A Coffee and Two Doghuts

When buying small items, water
that the modest advertisement
be trusted, two doughnuts for twelve cents
each, the allure of evening beverage
marked down to seventeen cents
at one cup of company; how desperate

to realize homelessness and poverty
in a world abundant made with
mountains, seas, trees and stars.
Where can one go without a dime except
to a taxi for the trust and withdraw
the pittances of a friend, a lover, a man,
who leaves me in his hospital bed, a strong hand, a steady stare.

Oh no, I'm not his air, I'm his fear.
water first,
spanish aires
firery arms
earth calm

or should water be last
before earth, air
fires, first

earth is not last
air is
spanish to then
fires become gutted.

earth
air
fire
water.

The world becomes the world goes on

Epithalamium

Damp by the trains
my sister has taken
a new rigidity since

her late marriage to August
upon the eve of deliquescence,
my father blossoms by the

nuptial, presented at Hugo's with
the same champagne I drink
this morning four years and

forty eight days later, to
their future prosperity, their past
bliss, their never-ending kiss.

Charles Olson was a thinker, a man skilled in letters and history, who had no patience with excess.

My father in contrast believes in analysis, one of the Italian vorticists, Giovanna Balla, who persists in domination of each instant, the horror and agony of his family.

Mr Olson, studying the traits of past civilizations discovered forms, methods of discourse that contradict his behavior, of dim brooding. Bad debts, electricity, women, taxes, prison terms, all facts Mr Olson scoffed my father idealizes and frets, not understanding the virtue of reception.

Of course, they never met. He loved my mother, from a distance, and I introduced them in Buffalo, at dinner in Onetta's Restaurant, on Main Street, where Mr Olson lived in 1965, next door at The University Motel. Then Professor of English at the State University of New York.

My father still chastises his memory.

It's very difficult for me to write of Professor Charles without the greatest love, and the most difficult honesty. Of course, my father is illiterate, and drug addicted, while Charles was clear and lucent in the time of greatest Trial.

His poetry shows that trial, that endurance, that deliberation to withstand the onslaught of immediate distraction. He worked amidst pressing problems, those that shall haunt our nation this decade, usury, negro riots, deceit and absolute fascism, parading under the guise of radical hubris.

Servants as my mother and father were failed to understand my devotion to a man who did not accept such conventions as their inabilities.

My mother more than compensated with her decision to labor in the best fashion she knew. And shortly followed Mr Olson to his death. Allowing hope for reunion of their opposite but strangely familiar goals. Long hours, love of children, notice of seasons, many friends and a gregarious, informative exchange marks both their memories. How we love being asked to remember them.

He was a democrat. Head of the Foreign Nationalities Committe under Franklin D. Roosevelt and she as well was a Democrat, passionately believing in such leaders as Adlai Stevenson, James Michael Curley and Leverett Saltonstall. He too spoke of the latter with respect, evidencing faith in poets, primes and future youth against the idiocy of my father, who was a patient in a mental asylum since my birth, convicted of murder, theft, and treason.

We three shine as beacons against his lingering months. Where the follies and predictions of his mother perpetrate themselves through his sodden corpse. Rotting in life for all my thirty odd years, and befouling desperate creation of this century the information available in both Mr Olson's and mother's achievement, as mathematician and prophet.

As a point of public testimony, Mr Olson skilled me in rhetoric and oratory, research, and gusto, the latter two qualities mother used, in conversation and argument.

How we talked together, sharing long hours of evening in hearing the sea, the birds and accents of eavesdroppers.

We were discreet, as we spent our desire in each other's riddance of interference. We went to movies, readings, auto-rides, museums, hotels, cities, on trains and picnics.

These facts occur in his poetry, as means of structure towards purchase of promise in the field of possible reward. Without our triple design, experience, a threat he largely received and she feared nonetheless embraced would be wasted. A vile thing my father threatens me with through police notice.

He abuses the law, while both of them revered it. I too am subject to their twin examples of celebration against public edifices, as the Fitz-Hugh Lane House in Gloucester, Massachusetts, the Pantheon in Rome and Frank Lloyd Wright's architectures.

Tall buildings frightened her. I adore them. Mr Olson took them for granted.

Newspapers pleased us. Good food a delight. Historical facts, while somewhat tedious to mother, propelled Charles to expound the details concurrent in actual execution.

Such as records of virgin discoveries, racial strife and Indian bestiality.

Her conversation came close to his. Mine is harder to voice. A small, simpering voice, inherited from drunks and con-men. Lisping sincerity to bogus heads of foreign powers in childlike indulgence.

They both died young at our hands. I was silly and idiotic. We were all frivolous. Chattering in opposite directions, planning ambitions none of us will destroy, sacred in celebration of love's serveillance.

An examination of behavior yields reasons. That is why I go with their histories. All of us born in winter or at least led to believe.

Without pedagoduery both Charles Olson and Anna Laffan worked to improve and instruct the youth of our era. They, one in doctrinaire of projective conception and the other, out of absolute despial towards despicable hypocrisy hoisted constant adherence to principles of scholarship, honesty, and togetherness.

There is no more pervertion than these American writers. 1st hand testimony on all of them confirms this, from themselves, their wives and lovers, and their work.

Charles and Mother faced them all, in past and future terms, never relenting in denial of their existence.

You're not worth the money,
you have got it.

Dartmouth Bus Boy

He stands in grandeur
upon an Upper East Side morning,
half-stiff
from impersonating many women the evening before,

in Scituate,
or a Washington court-house after
midnight, when fur
slung over the shoulder of a Greek harpsichord player

adorns Grandmother
at the keys near Marshfield. How well
she's done, with Cleopatra's gold choker
slung about her throat, and the droopy

ass of Barbara Bennett, in white silk slacks,
as Carol Lawrence, dance on glass.

On the era of a new age where peace beckons for thirty years and artists flourish everywhere in peace and harmony. Your machines are outdated and useless. Love blossoms in my heart like the face of an old friend glimpsed from another century. Until that time we may get together and share the apparition of our desire anywhere, hopeful against the observation of friends.

<u>2160</u>	=	Renaissance
-180		
1970	=	United States
<u>-180</u>		
1790	=	French Rev
<u>-180</u>		
1610	=	Cavaliers
<u>-180</u>		
1430	=	Chaucerian Age
<u>-180</u>		
1250		Dante
<u> 180</u>		
1070	=	Monasteries

From Shinnersberg to New York on Monday evening. Check luggage. Dine with DAVID then overnight. Afterwards walk down Park Avenue. Then out to Airport again.

The permanent style of elongation below the waist continues to stimulate man's talent, advanced through a demure visage, accentuated with paint, charcoal, and paste, both on the costume and apparel.

A bright black eye, a cinder style captures virtue, resulting in observation and annotated deeds.

Whether she has shoulders, a slip from Magnolia blossoms by Princess Hutton in a suit of Christian's, or an imitation from this week's graphic, I'll buy it.

Gold cuffs in a small fashion center on the seventh floor of this country's largest department store produces imports off boats over Berlin's long established priority to boost innovative processions in gowns, Victorian and Calvaric.

A silver cap de Buenos Aires. Molyneux, Caron. De Chirico, Chanel.

On the morning of September 22nd, 1970, in the Jordan Marsh Department Store, Massachusetts on the seventh floor Center, as announced in last month's issue, Vogue Fashion Across the Country in conjunction with three dozen other department stores throughout the country, arrived to perfect presentation.

Cardin black velvet, Givenchy design, a standard acccoutrement to harsh originals of unforgettable prideful ownership. A demure Sport pink, glamourized by a ruby and sapphire clip on the cowl emphasized the terribly over-wrought host, as mailed invitations unannounced in our broadsheet were required for entrance.

How distressing as your editor did not accept this stipulation since it was not printed.

A courrege's turban, Nina Ricci supper suits, Jenkins shopping ensemble, a Giorgio Sant Angelo dew flagrance in lemon and tangerine dotted the two-fisted observers.

Navy-blue blouse trimmed by Gothic tresses fascinated two colored performers who inquired whether in bold stance, I was a designer.

Yardly chapeux, a pre-midi Bébé frock of forest tone, Vienese couturier Mila Schon displayed prominently near the orchestra, as Elsa Triolet's midday sweatsuit on a devout Egyptian calmed the coffee-table throng. Pucci breakfast rayon, a Medic's cravat opened hostilities.

300 viewers noticed these standards. Modest harmonies of mauve, art nouveau purples Brussels leopards, excellent in combat, tablecloth bosoms, pinpointed the surprisingly strength of executive shades.

Polka dots and moonbeans, Dorthy weeping in the Southwest, Nancy bowing over couturiers, questioned the delay of parade of mannequins, as King Gustav VI Adolphus guarded his glances, directed to the balcony.

Perkins & Millet of UP also were brought down at the absence.

Simple Daché, a Mary Jane pattern commercialed the opening finally.

        Ethel pictures
              Topaz
          Balmain hoods
        presented the live
    from Madrid
          promenade
    shown on the screen

drew ennui, and should
not be reproduced in

our pages. Central Park
West furs strutted on

slides in my mind outside
the Dakota: Tintoretto

tassels, cherokee shawls
   glod ornaments, an El-

Khemi ncklace of ivory
   and turquoise, ostrich

feathers decorated
the announcement

print by Irving Penn /
David Bailey.

1. <u>Oyster Bay</u>
   Calvin Klein - Originalia

2. <u>Spanish</u> fox
   Donald Brooks
   scarf Paolo of Elizabeth A.
   from Canada

3. Town and Country

4. Kaspar houndstooth
   check, gabardine

5. Morgan Memorial
   Salvation Army
   Peggy Miller

6. Tico riding dog
   Eva Braun's hair

7. Bill Blass beret out of
   the Sorbonne sewer gray
   shirt and tunic matching

8. Anginalia boredom
   on false fronts

9. Tie and blouse by
   Paisley

10. Hattie Carnegie
    modeled by Mrs
    Burr of Dorset violets
    and glasses in cookie
    cut.

11. Kaspar Kentucy
    tweeds jived with
    previous dark imposition

12. Bill Blass turned
    left except for the braid of
    Great Danish trellises

13. Toque Emba
    of Munich gait.

14. Cheap accessories

15. Arnaud Rodriguez

    confused us in excellent
    pattern.

16. Real sleek garment
    from Algeria.

17. Syrian import
    modeled by Inigo.

18. Mediterranean
    Emb-glow knit wool by
    Jerry Silverman

19. White hat and shiny
    bag and shiny shoe of
    Scott

20. Nylon stockings
    by Saint Laurent and
    jaws of svelte

21. Pauline Trigère
    matron

22. Lace brim
    Caperzio

23. Algiers aristocracy
    of jasper, mink

    snood.

24. Lincoln Hussar
    discharged
    the endless exhibition

25. Civic band buttons
    Yves

26. Fontana

    from Da Vinci

27. Red white and black
    pink scarlet
    chamber duties

28. Jerry Silverman
    in boots
    and riding plumes

29. Gothic rails on
    cotton devotion

30. Poncho dress

31. Greek dignity

32. Jumpsuit of
    Marseilles beans

33. Hebrew hotshot
    lizard belt

34. Donaval tweed
    and jersey, a little
    shoulder sheltering shawl
    high waist with excellent
    gold platinum from
    Araby

35. Sparkling May
    du Bois Adam Charles

36. Piranesi Nuremberg
    Bodice and adorable scholarship

37. Berlin peasant
    politess

38. Donald Brooks
    serene quiet silver
    backles on SL pumps

39. Umnamble elegance

40. Paris hedonism
    with hefty Georgian
    declasse minus
    under clothes

41. In the clutter
    Germany forgot

42. Austria memories
    flowed in fine taste

43. Maroon hapsbergs
    patterned out

44. Brighton philo
    matheia dowagers
    kept in Chestnut

45. Malcolm Charles
    liberty whole wrap

46. Courreges in
    monastery patrol.
    "That's" very Dior, according to
    our commentor, Mrs

47. Striped knit from
    matte

48. Paton or Maggy Rouf
    in imitation hosery

49. Satin tailoring
    of bridal fleece

50. Diamond girdle
    strawberries

51. Bonnie Cashin
    by Phoebe MacAdams
    of Colorado

52. Debut Harrow.

53. An Atlanta pantaloon.

54. Elgin bo-peep
    from California

55. Trim disciplined
    of crystal.

56 Coins by Joan
    Leslie and
    ensemble of fleurs-de lis.

57. the handsome
    salon of French
    petit trianon

58. Silk ribboned diamonds
    on Monet boots and gloves

59. Le Grand Trianon
    in narcissus peacock

60. Asymetry

61. Deshabille brown

62. Flame pajamas

63. Soft jersey,
    royal blue ribbons

64. Polish Po.
    Warsaw

65. Oscar La Renta
    stained glass Giovanni
    Buonarroti.

66. Adelle Davis of
    Elizabethean favorites.

67. The ruffled collar
    of Flemish lace

68. Medway plaster.

69. Godey's Endurance

70. Mrs Burr
    in velvet.

71. Christian Dior

72. Adele Simpson

73. Oscar de La Renta's
    pedestrianism

74. Smoky cocco and girl
    from Toyko

75. Hamish Mori
    gold

76. Worth – Je Reiens

76. Vers A Toi.

77. trouser of
    Constantinople diaplomas

78. Crêpe of
    impeccable veiling by
    Thelma Ryan

79. Gilt cord

80. Preserved teas
    and pastettes

81. Post-minus
    gowns for
    the ball.

Edward Thommen

At <u>lunch,</u> DANK EXCEPT FOR MENIL
remembered from its cold chilled
display, through his generosity,

although we chose a well-lit
booth, expensively-papered wall,
the <u>diners</u> broke ice, rudely installed

purposely to annoy our spell
at being together, and hoping well
towards china, menu and its help.

It remained sparse until
the table left, under bail, out for a new trial,
maliced from unsuspected animosity

upon we three, father, son and brother,
kept together by choice of one another.
Little did Edward realize, or Nikolai consider

any importance attached to the rendez-vous,
often celebrated in story and anecdote, where
friends recollect to evenings of song or supper

over checkered table-cloths, leather cushions
wooden partitions, inexpensive moderation
catering to federal coterie and powder buffoons.

             -J
             5.10.1971

The following poems, lists and notes begin at the back of the journal and run counter to the main body of the text from back to front. They were written upside down and mostly on the verso page, usually left blank elsewhere in the notebook.

TOMESOD

In the window's
golden reflection

E.K.

10:35

10:10

715 Summer St
Brookline Mass 02051

1: Subscribe to <u>Women's Wear Daily</u>

2: Appt for Hair at 77

3: Tooth filling

4. False plates

5. pay bill for groceries ,15

and dinner 3.00

6. Tax ...   3 ...
                dollars

7. Observe : Arts = article
                to dividends

1. It won't let me go whatever

he sells the house or not.

Anyone can do that
but you wont be around to
                find out
I dont even know
how to kiss you.

Reaction

They must let us know you
I am the chase and you are pursuit.

At one time, on Monday morning the roads were quiet. On either side of the drive to town, graceful silent meadows undulated to the hill built to withstand the sea, peaceful and sluggish drifting past the land.

Grass and trim shrubbery were placed at convenient places over the slopes. Expensive loam and soil blossomed under the summer month, and the gentle blue heaven blessed the beneficent area by politesse and prim observance.

A TAILORING COSTUME

<u>Notes</u>
to the lecture you're going to hear this morning by Mr A Bach.

1. on the prig – the professional

Would you please explain how to alter narrow shoulders if full-
busted?

2. a cutting board

3. a stretch tape measure

(4. We did spend two Christmas dinners together.

    butter butter bottom of
           the ladder)

   tape measure bosom
4. indentation
5. derriere

Lord and Taylor

She is awfully fat and her legs
          are withered

ribbons, silk dresses, hose, laces, rings.

Imported foods keep them in business

front square on fold, three dots on
   ~~fold~~ —

Sporting fabric is like doing a water color close-up.

a 5 8 seam

a guage
a seam-guide

this curve, that curve

he does open the mail and he does read it—.

I have no clothes and no money either.

:Resolution. To attend a fashion show here.

Sewing is not a book. It's a mechanical thing, like playing the piano.

I do not go for crowd movements.

I'm in real white and blue and I always shall be no matter what I have on.

He is a soldier from the second World War.

6.
When you touch a pattern to fabric, you pin it right.

1942   at   a year   old

5 . 6 .   seams

   2 hems

Plaza 3 -

Bergdorf Goodman   for men

Alida van Altenberg

Simone Signoret – Casque d'Or
~~Zza Zza~~

Jeanette McDonald – Nelson Eddy
Irene Dunne – Dr. Francis Griffith
Virginia McMath = Ginger Rodgers
                    Fred Astaire

Barbara Stanwyck –
                    Martha Vickers

Seen or encountered in Boston

Jean Seberg in a blue coat on Stuart Street, Steve McQueen in hot
pursuit; Gloria Swanson at Filene's cut shortly after Michele
Morgan arrived avec D.D. Babs Stanwyck bypassed in shocking
silk
      Meg O'Brien last evening at Ken's before Tom Jones
barstooling :::: the Empress Seliene accompagné H.K.H. Prins
demand encore dejeunée.

Linda Lovely
Beverly Collins
Joanne Kyger
Shirley Berman
Freude Mittleman
Joanne Meister
Tina Meltzer
Joanne Doyle
Louise Hermes
Nemi Frost 10
Anne Frost
Eloise Mixon
Sheila Plumb devine Jones
Ronnie Levin
Jan Balas
Jan Minsk
Sheila Carter
Bette Richer
Sharon Morrill
Sharon Fontana 20
Sue d'Angulo
Joan Brown
Jay de Feo
Joanne McClure
Ruth Weiss
Patty Topalian
Mrs. Driscoll
Cameron
Gogo Nesbitt 30
Sheila Rochbloom Harmer
Joelle Swayze
Lee Dabney
Francine
Loy Lee
Madeline Gleason
Helen Adam

Ruth de Witt Diamant
Dora Dull Fitzgerald
Caroline Dunn 40
Bobbie Louise Hall
Ida Hodes
Celeste Turner Wright
Helene Dorn
Elseue Sorrentino
Ina Mursk
Sally Hoyem
Timotha Doane
Kate Mulholland
Diane di Prima 50
Mrs Richard Baker
Sheila Albany
Mad Rita
Christopher MacLaine's girl
Mrs Richard Brautigan
Mrs Russ Tamblyn
Gloria Stockwell
Diana Hadley
Dorinda Dixon
Helen Sullivan 60
Sheila Weslauski
Rita Joyce
Ann Joyce
Barbara Smith
Mary Smith
Mary Watson
Nancy Watson
Ellen Watson
Joan Corcoran
Elaine Wilson 70
Pat Reardon
Ruth Mackin
Phyllis Monroe

Mary Barrett
Helen Barrett
Joan Barrett
Helen Vickerson
Jane Vickerson
Arlene Ladden
Eila Kokkinen 80
Panna Grady
Sandra Hochman
Phoebe MacAdams
Sara Schrom
Nancy White
Terese Bartollotta
Teresa van Volkenberg
Susan Cummings
Marie MacDermott
Peggy Laffan 90
Arlene Meedham
Johanna Dochy
Jane Christy
Drue Heigy
Melanie York
Mrs Robert Hahn
Joan Ford
Mrs Myles Slater
Mrs Tom Clark
Mrs David Posner 100
Lady Mary Wedgwood
Mrs Edith Mittner
Mrs Cyril McCoy
Mrs Jos Condon, Jr.
Kate Williams
Emily Cheney
Terry Gibbs
Mary Kerkorian
Sylvia Palter

Eleonara McKay 110
Christina Cummings
Mrs Ellen Needham
Mrs Edw F Binley
Beth Sach
Mrs Sach
Mrs Dochy
Mrs Thomas McDermott
Helena Nally
Helena Callaghan
May Beach 120
Mrs Chas Plymell
Helen Jales
Patsy Nally
Rosemary Nally
Fay Spain
Mrs Marie Reynolds
Mrs Clare
Mrs Geraldine O'Donovan
Sandy Berrigan
Mgt. De Cholnoky 130
Phyllis Braemer
Mrs Nellie Reddington
Janet McGrath
Eleanor McGrail
Mae McKinnon
Marion Wieners
Rita McIntire
Anne McCabe
Dot Fleming
M.C. Richards 140
Nancy Richards
Barbara Douglas
Janet Nilon
Bunny McKinnon
Constance Witcox

Kate Bunker
Polly Brown
Kristen Hall
Joan Mitchell
Barbara Guest 150
Priscilla Moyan
Vera Dorina
Patricia de Loach
Barbara de Loach
Bonnie Bremser
Joby Kelly
Jean Radoslovich
Mary Shore Ferrini
Mrs Irving Sanger
Marisol 160
Nico
Ivy Nicholson
Mrs Hugh Auchincloss
Amy Levin
Rita Liff
May Conway
Helen Vendler
Anne Barrett
Mrs Mary Barrett
Gert Loyons 170
Joanne Howard
Anne Simon
Rona Page
Christen Miller
Martha Davis
Mrs Gerald van de Wiele
Mary Fiore
Mrs Nell Rice
Elaine Chamberlain
Hilda Morley 180
Mary Heminway

Nancy Wilson-Ross
Dathys Terrell
Diana Jay
Meredith Taggard
Marianne Moore
Galen Williams
Mrs Karl Gay
190 Mrs Melissa Benter
Nina Laffan
Muriel Rukeyser
Denise Levertov
Helen Chasin
Elsa Dorfman
Jeanne Broburg
Mrs Richard Brooks
Barbara Kahan
Janet Cooper
Madelyn Davis 200
Helen Kleist
Liz van den Bencken
Veronique Alewyn
Marjorie Benjamin
Elaine Spears
Erin Matson
Dorothy White
Hettie Cohen
Ann Parsons
Carol Senacle 210
Elizabeth Gross
Diana Starling
Cosima Cosmo
Princess Alica Paolozzi
Julie Lawrence
V.R. Lang
Catherine Huntington
Helen Neville

Mrs Tom Clark 210
Debbie Caen
Benedetta Barzini
Joanna Hutchins
May Sarton
Lynn Fisher
Mrs Rattray
Blanche Bigelow
Eleo Curtis
Ellen Neville
Celeste Neville 220
Suzanne Neville
Janet Neville
Linda Ross
Barbara Ross
Mrs Walter Ross
Mrs Ruth Hepelin
Mrs Leonard Malone
Mrs Michael Murphy
Eleanor Murphy
Nancy Callaghan 230
Helen Lawless
Mrs John Smith
Mary Greeley
Kathleen Needham
Margaret Fieldler
Mrs Haler
Diedre Hutton
Brenda Buillion
Martha Dubois
Mary Ryan 240
Ida Tierney
Jane Murphy
Florence Landry
Helen Hennessey
Teressa Pineault

Bernadette Pineault
Mrs W.J. Pineault
Betina Hennessey
    Foyle
Kitty Murphy
Mary Ann de Pietro 250
Ann Marie Desmond
Anne Leiffer
Nancy Swain
Dorothy Haus
Mrs Barrett
Jane Bartay
Mrs Taylor
Bernadette Meyer
B — Baker
Mina Loy's daughter 260
Beatrice Paipert 261
Lois Lunt
Ann La Hive
Louise Van Ham
Ann Lynch
Priscilla Welch
Barbara Durkee
Linda Harrison
Eleanor Brown 269
Mary Wieners 270
Mary Brown
Anne Waldman
Jeane Edelman
Rosemary Proust
Fernanda Southeys
Joan Wilentz
Mina Mencken
Mrs Fred Cassirer
Priscilla Urbanek
Grace Hartigan 280

Nell Blaine
Elaine de Kooning
Bettita Sutherland
Pat Rosen
Mrs Axelrod
Mrs Rudolph Wieners
Agnes Steglish
Helen Malinowski
Mrs Ralph de Gruttola
Carol Weston
<u>290</u>
Liz Harlech
Louise de la Fey
Jane Ormsly Gore
The Countess of Gowrie - Xandra
                          Binghampton
Mrs Wynn Chamberlain
Ruth Landshoff Yorck
Edith Sedgwick
Brigit Berlin
Mitzi Shauggnessy
Patsy Shauggnessy 300
Ann Ribbon
Filmaker friend of Allen's
Dolly Bolton   303
Mrs

Poets I Have Met

1. Leonard McCarthy S.J.
   Loker Raley
   Francis Sweeney S.J.
   Terence Connolly S.J.
   Joseph Dunn
   Stephen Jonas
   Edward Marshall
   Charles Olson
   Edward Dorn
   Michael Rumaker
   Jonathan Williams
   Denise Levertov
   Harry Kemp
   Frank O'Hara
   Robin Blaser
   Jack Spicer
   Lyon Phelps
   V.R. Lang
   Hugh Amory
20. Barbara Guest
   John La Touche
   James Schuyler
   George Montgomery
   Edwin Denby
   Robert Duncan
   Robert Creeley
   Tony Landreau
   Wallace Berman
   John Reed
   John Chance
   John Davidson
   Robert Nichols
   Ruth Weiss
   Lawrence Ferlinghetti

Gary Snyder
Philip Whalen
Robert Kaufman
Celeste Turner Wright
Stephen Spender
40. Roberts Blossom
I.E. Alexander
Edwin Muir
James Merrill
Eleo Curtis
Blanche Bigelow
Allen Ginsberg
Peter Orlovsky
Jack Kerouac
Shig Murayäo
Hilda Morley
Daniel Moore
Robert Lowell
Anne Sexton
Daniel Zimmerman
Michael Levinson
Albert Glover
Fred Wah
Harvey Brown
60 Bill Berkson
Kenneth Koch
John Ashbery
A.B. Spellman
Leroi Jones
Gilbert Sorrentino
Joel Oppenheimer
William Burroughs
Al Fowler
Clive Matson
Ray Bremser
Allen de Loach

David Schaff
Bill Margolis
Ingeborg Bachman
Ted Hughes
David Posner
David Rattray
Ed Sanders
Louis Simpson
80. Joanne Kyger
Harold Dull
George Stanley
Ebbe Borregaard
Stan Persky
Don Allen
Gerard Malanga
Anne Waldman
Lewis MacAdams
John Godfrey
Ruth Yorck
Marianne Moore
W.H. Auden
Willard Maas
George Barker
John Logan
Edward Lucie-Smith
George MacBeth
David Waggoner
Dorothy Van Ghent
100 Sam Loveman
Muriel Rukeyser
Salvatore Quasimdo
Pablo Neruda
Yevgeni Vevtenshenko
Ezra Pound
James Schevill
Robin Skelton

George Oppen
Louis Zukovsky
Josephine Miles
Madeline Gleason
Helen Adam
John Berryman
Leslie Fiedler
Irving Feldman
Mac Hammond
Lawrence Osgood
Robert Kelly
120 Anthony Hecht
John Hall Wheelock
Howard Moss
Archibald MacLeish
Rev. Jakob Lind
Gunther Gräss
Carl Weiss
Mary Beach
Claude Pelieu
Maurice Girdodias
Gogo Nesbitt
Philip Lamantia
Charles Henri-Ford
David Haselwood
Kirby Doyle
Michael McClure
Irving Rosenthal
Arthur Kopit
Tom Wolfe
140 Paul Krassner
Gregory Corso
Seymour Krim
Allen Katzman
Ted Wilentz
Helen Chasin

Susan Sherman
Diane di Prima
Diane Wakosi
Rochelle Owens
Richard Brautigan
Jerome Rothenberg
Armand Schwerner
Charles Simic
Samuel French Morse ~~(have not met)~~
Richard Wilbur
Richard Eberheart
Philip Booth
May Swenson
160 May Sarton
Gerrit Lansing
T.S. Eliot
E.E. Cummings
Elliott Coleman
Victor Coleman
Bill Hutton
Johannes Edfelt
Delmore Schwartz
Paul Goodman
Herbert Huncke
Bonnie Bremser
172 Janine Pommey-Vega
Parker Tyler
Charles Plymell
Daniel Dwyer S.J.
Daniel Bergigan S.J.
John l'Heureux S.J.
Sister Mary Korte
George Plympton
180 The Earl of Gowie, Greysteil
Louise Glück
Wynn Chamberlain

Jack Micheline
Jack Hirschman
Ronald Duncan
James Liddy
Roy Kiyooka
Stanton Hoffman
Jean Garrigue
Dylan Thomas
Gene Derwood
Alvin Landry
Ann Landon
Carolyn Kizer
Andrew Hoyem
Sanders Russell
{ Brother Antoninus
Landis Everson
200 William Everson
Phyllis Webb
George Seferis
John Malcolm Brinnin
Kimon Friar
Kirby Congdon
Jay Socin
John Taggard
Walter Lowenfels
Paul Blackburn
Carol Bergé
Alex Weiner
Miroslav Holub
André Frenaud
Tony Towle
Frank Lima
William Wantling
Vincent Ferrini
Jerome Mazzaro
Ted Berrigan

Parade

On Forty-Second Street, a sidewalk café
at noon provides rest and water
against the ceaseless rush of workers
out of shops and offices always

well dressed to raise the vision
of visitors, walking to spend the day before
the bus home to work; after a benefit for friends,
or at a night of theatre watching a proven draw
perform the work of legend. Until evening falls

midtown, the mahagonny bars remain with whiskey and women

to once more open the doors of Manhattan to
strange young men from out of town
who fill the sidewalks with lost addresses,
and left over make-up, perhaps in too-tight shoes

having spent the dawn friendless though found
the city rich uptown at some elegant hotel,
crossing lobbies past a Veronese dining room
to catch the newest show, the dirtiest look.

the affair is better
left right there
the matter over

the matter is better
left right there
jungle behavior
seems

the affair is better
left right there
unstated though enacted
over thoroughfare

1921   1922   1923   1924   1925

1926   1927   1928   1929   1930
                                                          pablum

1931   1932   1933   1934   1935

1936	1937	1938	1939	1940
	a baby brother	~~potence~~		~~potence~~

1941	1942	1943	1944	1945
a spotless	garage			food
house	pajamas			
a faultless	a stocking			

living room
a clean dining room
and spic bedrooms
Neat toilet and adequate kitchen.
a back porch
Clean window rooms.

44

24

48

22

1946	1947	1948	1949	1950
graduation				graduation
presents				presents

1951	1952	1953	1954
			graduation
			presents

| 1955 | 1956 | 1957 | 1958 |
| | | visits | |

1959	1960	1961	1962
clothes	books	books	Theatre tickets
food	visits	suit (with Princess	(with Princess Anne)
money	hospitalization	bathrobe	Anne)
	~~(1000 dollars)~~	pajamas	~~ignorance~~
	cigarettes (Benson	cards	~~questions~~
	N.Y. Times & Hedges)	(1000 dollars	
	ice cream	treatments)	
	pajamas	rosary beads	
	bathrobe	~~typewriter~~	

1963	1964	1965
cards	birthday present	travel money
visits	cash	food
transportation	records	cards
dinner	~~sweat~~	~~cash~~
file cabinet (with Princess Anne)		visits
cash	sweater	phone calls
~~sweat~~	(with Princess Anne)	tie sack
	movie tickets	sheets
	shirts	shirts
	shorts	ties
	trousers	stockings
		trousers
		sweater

Linda Edmund, Jr

Mr. Thomas Callaghan
Nisse Statement Commission
Logan Airport
East Boston, Massachusetts

1963	1964	1965
suit	visits	packages
Navel money		cash
shoes	S A F	cards
visits	Ed Sanders	letters
food		visits
	Expo	

Presents My Mother Gave Me

1969	1970
visits	bedspreads
a briefcase	curtains
a white shirt	meals
2 ties	cigarettes
1 stocking cap	magazines
stockings	food
50 letters	cash
cash	bus tickets
rugs	birthday cash
shades	driving lessons
wallpaper	cake
a room	pills
part of the house	food for friends
pillows	
mattress	
spring	
cigarettes	
driving lessons	
pills	
underwear	

Plus Mine

Just sit there. If you do the thing
I will charge you for it. I have
never subjected you to one thing

I'd rip that that silly suit
off his bare breast.

At the Oriental Theatre, always be sure.

To Louisa
From John
for her collection.

John Wieners was born in Milton, Massachusetts in 1934 to Albert Eugene and Anna Elizabeth (Laffan) Wieners. He attended St. Gregory's in Dorchester, MA and Boston College High School. From 1950-1954 he studied at Boston College, where he earned his A.B. In 1954 he heard Charles Olson read at the Charles Street Meeting House on Beacon Hill in the midst of a hurricane. He decided to enroll at Black Mountain College where he studied under Olson and Robert Duncan from 1955 to 1956. He then worked as an actor and stage manager at the Poet's Theater in Cambridge, and began to edit *Measure*, releasing three issues over the next several years.

From 1958 to 1960 he lived in San Francisco and actively participated in the San Francisco Poetry Renaissance. *The Hotel Wentley Poems* was published in 1958, when Wieners was twenty-four.

Wieners returned to Boston in 1960 and was institutionalized. In 1961 he moved to New York City and worked as an assistant bookkeeper at Eighth Street Books from 1962-1963, living on the Lower East Side with Herbert Huncke. He went back to Boston in 1963, employed as a subscriptions editor for Jordan Marsh department stores until 1965. Wieners' second book, *Ace of Pentacles*, was published in 1964.

In 1965, after traveling with Olson to the Spoleto Festival and the Berkeley Poetry Conference, he enrolled in the Graduate Program at SUNY Buffalo. He worked as a teaching fellow under Olson, then as an endowed Chair of Poetics, staying until 1967, with *Pressed Wafer* coming out the same year. In the spring of 1969 Wieners was again institutionalized, and wrote *Asylum Poems*.

Nerves was released in 1970, containing work from 1966 to 1970. In the early 1970s Wieners became active in education and publishing cooperatives, political action committees, and the gay liberation movement. He also moved into an apartment at 44 Joy Street on Beacon Hill, where he lived for the next thirty years.

In 1975 *Behind the State Capitol or Cincinnati Pike* was published, a magnum opus of "Cinema decoupages; verses, abbreviated prose insights." For the next ten years he published rarely and remained largely out of the public eye.

Black Sparrow Press released two collections edited by Raymond Foye, *Selected Poems: 1958-1984* and *Cultural Affairs in Boston*, in 1986 and 1988 respectively. A previously unpublished journal by Wieners came out in 1996, entitled *The Journal of John Wieners is to be called 707 Scott Street for Billie Holliday 1959*, documenting his life in San Francisco around the time of *The Hotel Wentley Poems*.

At the Guggenheim in 1999 Wieners gave one of his last public readings, celebrating an exhibit by the painter Francesco Clemente. A collaboration between the two, *Broken Woman*, was also published.

Wieners died on March 1, 2002 at Massachusetts General Hospital, having collapsed a few days previously after an evening attending a party with his friend and publisher Charley Shively. *Kidnap Notes Next*, a collection of poems and journal entries, was published posthumously in 2002.

Michael Carr was born in 1978 and is the author of *Platinum Blonde* (Fewer & Further) and *Softer White* (House Press). He co-edited a chapbook of work by the early twentieth-century poet Samuel Greenberg, *Self Charm: Selected Sonnets & Other Poems*. With Dorothea Lasky he edits Katalanché Press. Since 1999 he has lived in Cambridge, Massachusetts.

will promote renewed peace and perceptive pleasure. Programs will be less theoretical and provide for adventurous paths to the everyday pursuits in the accepted patterns of existence.

Imagination will be more pervasive and progress made in travel over ocean and space. Dress asymmetrical and modes of greeting and conversation elliptical and extreme bizarreness absent except in bigness, mammoth grandeur of architecture and color. Music string and forms of verse controlled symbolism